Mules & More

*40 Craft Breweries
Share Signature Beer Cocktails*

by
Steve Akley
&
Lee Ann Sciuto

Mules & More

40 Craft Breweries Share Signature Beer Cocktails

Written by:
Steve Akley
& Lee Ann Sciuto

Published by:
S.A.P. Entertainment

To the Hopheads Everywhere:

While there is nothing like a bottle or glass of beer, it sure is nice to see beer finally playing in the cocktail arena as well!

Introduction

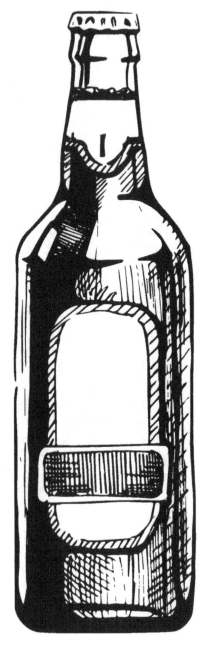

Mules & More
40 Craft Breweries Share Signature Beer Cocktails

Introduction by Steve Akley, Author

Moscow/Kentucky Mule

1.5 ounces vodka (bourbon for Kentucky Mule)
1 tsp. lime juice
4 ounces ginger beer
Lime slice
Sprig of mint (Kentucky Mule only)

Pour vodka and lime juice in copper mug.

Fill with crushed ice and top off with ginger beer.

Garnish with lime and sprig of mint.

While there have always been a handful of cocktails involving beer (the Irish Car Bomb for instance), they really didn't become popular until the Moscow Mule, a cocktail tracing its roots back to the 1940s, was revived in the early 2000s. Once the Moscow Mule became a staple of cocktail enthusiasts, bartenders began exploring more cocktail ideas with beer.

Breweries have also taken note of this trend. Rather it's through their own tasting room, or via beer cocktail recipes shared on their website, there are more beer cocktails now than ever before.

Mules & More takes a look at 40 craft breweries and the signature beer cocktail they use to highlight the offerings from their respective companies. You will find a diverse mixture of cocktails here that run the gamut from simple offerings for the novice bartender to complex builds that would challenge even the most experienced mixologist.

The end result is a fun exploration of how creative you can get with beer in cocktails.

Cheers!

Table of Contents

The Signature Cocktails 11

  7 Mile Brewery (Rio Grande, NJ) 12

    7 Mile Mint Mule 13

  16 Mile Brewing Company (Georgetown, DE) 14

    Bourbon Sunshine 15

  32 North Brewing Co. (San Diego, CA) 17

    Tequila Weisse 18

  Abbey of the Holy Goats Brewery (Roswell, GA) 19

    Gardentini 20

  Absolution Brewing Company (Torrance, CA) 21

    Absolution Old Fashioned 22

  Aleman Brewing Company (Chicago, IL) 24

    The Lawnmower Man 25

  Aloha Beer Company / The HI Brau Room (Honolulu, HI) ...27

    Barley Squared 28

  Alulu Brew Pub (Chicago, IL) 29

    Epishelf Marquee 30

  Anderson Valley Brewing Company (Booneville, CA) 31

    Holy Mule 32

  Argyle Brewing Company (Greenwich, NY) 34

    The Candy Corn 35

  Bear Bones Beer (Lewiston, ME) 37

    Coffee & C.R.E.A.M. 38

  Belching Beaver Tavern & Grill (Vista, CA) 40

    The Bitter Truth 41

  Cape Cod Beer (Hyannis, MA) 43

    Cape & Islands Punch 44

  Cinder Block Brewery (North Kansas City, MO) 46

Cherry Pit 47

Combustion Brewery & Taproom (Pickerton, OH) 48

Beer Mimosa Flight...49

Crane Brewing Company (Raytown, MO) 51

Orchards of Plenty..52

Demented Brewing Company (Middlesex, NJ)....................53

Orcus Old Fashioned 54

Deschutes Brewery (Bend, OR) 56

Black Butte Bloody Mary 57

Dry Dock Brewing Company (Aurora, CO)...........................59

Apricolada..60

Empirical Brew Pub (Chicago, IL)..62

Gamma Mule 63

Firetrucker Brewery (Ankeny, IA) 65

German Chocolate Cake Porter...66

Foothills Brewing (Winston-Salem, NC)..............................68

The Pacific Jade 69

Forbidden Root Restaurant and Brewery (Chicago, IL).......71

The Rake 72

Friendship Brewing Company (Wentzville, MO) 73

Friendship Recovery 74

Half Day Brewing Co. (Lincolnshire, IL)..............................75

Iron Horse Coffee Porter Café 76

Heavy Seas Alehouse Baltimore (Baltimore, MD) 78

Southern Cross 79

Jolly Pumpkin Artisan Ales (Dexter, MI) 81

Bam Shandy 82

Left Hand Brewing Company (Longmont, CO).....................84

Good Juju Moscow Mule..85

Logboat Brewing Co. (Columbia, MO).................................87

   Turtle Power!...88

Maui Brewing Co. / Waikiki Pub (Honolulu, HI) 90

   Bahama Mana 91

Midnight Sun Brewing Company (Anchorage, AK).............93

   Trick'd Out Old Fashioned..94

Outlaw Brewing Company (Winchester, NH).......................95

   The Ultimate Enticement...96

Red Clay Brewing Company (Opelika, AL)..........................97

   Red Clay Peach Sour 98

Revolution Brewing (Chicago, IL)......................................99

   Kentucky Rosa 100

SanTan Brewing Company (Chandler, AZ) 102

   SanTan Arizona Mule 103

Square One Brewery (St. Louis, MO)...............................104

   Breakfast Beer 105

Sun King Brewery (Indianapolis, IN)................................107

   Pachangarita 108

ThirstyBear Brewing Company (San Francisco, CA) 110

   Beer Cocktail #18..111

Twisted Spike Brewing Company (Oklahoma City, OK) 113

   Beermosa...114

Voodoo Brewery (Meadville, PA) 116

   Met-Mosa...117

Resources...118

Websites of Featured Breweries 119

Photo Credits 124

About the Authors 125

    Steve Akley 126

        Find Steve on Social Media 126

    Lee Ann Sciuto 127

Steve's Other Works 128

Special Thanks 129

    Much Appreciation for Those That Helped 130

The Signature Cocktails

7 Mile Brewery

3156 Route 9 South
Rio Grande, New Jersey 08242
(609) 365-7777

7milebrew.com
info@7milebrew.com

Established
2016

Leadership
Pete Beyda, Owner
Chris Collett, Owner
Mark Demberger Jr, Sales Director
Alex Paul, Head Brewer
Bill Simmons, Assistant Brewer

7 Mile Mint Mule

When the 7 Mile Brew Crew was challenged to come up with an original Mule recipe, using one of their own products, it was quickly determined that El Heffe Hefeweizen would be selected for the task. It was released shortly after the brewery opened in September of 2016, and quickly became one of the signature seasonal beers. After a few tasty concoctions, the recipe for the 7 Mile Mint Mule was determined to be a very light, refreshing, and crushable Mule!

Submitted by: 7 Mile Brew Crew at 7 Mile Brewery

Serve in a copper mug

Ingredients:
- 4 fresh mint leaves
- 2 lime wedges
- ¾ ounce of ginger liqueur
- 6 ounces of 7 Mile Brewery El Heffe Hefeweizen Beer
- Ice
- 1 lime pinwheel and a sprig of fresh mint for garnish

Preparation:
1. In a traditional copper Moscow Mule mug, lightly muddle two lime wedges and 4 leaves of fresh mint.
2. Top muddled ingredients with ice packed to rim of mug.
3. Add ginger liqueur and top off with beer.
4. Lightly stir cocktail as to mix, but not disturb the carbonation.
5. Garnish cocktail with fresh sprig of mint and lime pinwheel.

16 Mile Brewing Company

413 S. Bedford Street
Georgetown, Delaware 19947
(302) 253-8816

16milebrewery.com

Established
2009

Leadership
Brett McCrea

Bourbon Sunshine

This is customer service at its finest. Owner Brett McCrea was talking to a customer one night whose regular drink was the Amber Sun. He knew about the infusion process and asked what Brett thought of bourbon and peaches being added to his favorite beer. Brett, being a bourbon enthusiast, happily trialed a small batch and it turned out splendidly.

This is a recipe for the beer-brewing cocktail enthusiast as it involves making and kegging a beer. Once you make it, you have your cocktail on tap, though!

Submitted by: Brett McCrea

Serve in a pint glass

Ingredients:
- 2-Row malted barley
- Dark crystals
- Malted wheat
- The-best-bourbon-you-can-get-your-hands-on
- Canned peaches in heavy syrup
- All-spice and cinnamon for a spiced finish

Preparation:
1. This brew is a based on 16 Mile Brewery's Amber Sun Amber Ale.
2. It is made and then keged two weeks to a month later.
3. During the kegging process it is infused with the bourbon, the peaches and however much of the spice you'd like to include.

Bourbon Sunshine
by 16 Mile Brewery

32 North Brewing Co.

8655 Production Avenue, Suite A
San Diego, California 92121
(619) 323-2622

32northbrew.com
info@32northbrew.com

Established
2014

Leadership
Steve Peterson

Tequila Weisse

The sourness in the cocktail comes entirely from the beer, and it made a pretty fantastic drink.

Submitted by: 32 North Brewing Co.

Serve in a rocks glass

Ingredients:

- 2 ounces tequila
- 2 ounces simple syrup
- 4 ounces Pomegranate Landfall Berliner Weisse
- 2 dashes of bitters
- ½ of a lime
- Mint leaves

Preparation:

1. Squeeze a half lime into a shaker.
2. Add ice, tequila, simple syrup, and bitters in the shaker and shake.
3. Pour into rocks glass.
4. Top with Pomegranate Landfall Berliner Weisse.
5. Garnish with fresh mint leaves.

Abbey of the Holy Goats Brewery

4000 Northfield Way, Suite 800
Roswell, Georgia 30076
(470) 282-1444

abbeyoftheholygoats.com
info@abbeyoftheholygoats.com

Established
2016

Leadership
Kathy Davis, Owner

Gardentini

Highly aromatic with a light and refreshing taste, without sweetness, and a dry finish.

Submitted by: Kathy Davis, Abby of the Holy Goats Brewery

Serve in a 8 ½ ounce coupe glass

Ingredients:

- 1 ½ ounces of Cocchi Americano
- 1 basil leaf
- Goats in the Garden Saison
- Lemon twist

Preparation:

1. Add Cocchi Americano to cocktail shaker with basil leaf and ice.
2. Shake and strain into a 8 ½ ounce coupe glass.
3. Top with Goats in the Garden and a lemon twist.

Absolution Brewing Company

2878 Columbia Street
Torrance, California 90503
(310) 490-4860

absolutionbrewingcompany.com
info@absolutionbrewingcompany.com

Established
2013

Leadership
Nigel Heath
Steve Farguson

Absolution Old Fashioned

The addition of maraschino cherry juice and burnt orange peel to Absolution's very popular barrel-aged beer enhances the nuances of the oak and bourbon and softens the hops resulting in a wonderful and complex mouthfeel. Yummy!

Submitted by: Absolution Brewing Company

Serve in a beer tulip/goblet

Ingredients:

- Absolution American Revelation (bourbon barrel-aged RyePA)
- Splash of maraschino cherry juice
- Burnt/Flamed orange peel
- Maraschino cherry garnish

Preparation:

1. Add cherry juice to glass.
2. Fill glass with beer.
3. Add flamed orange peel and maraschino cherry for garnish.

Absolution Old Fashioned
by Absolution Brewing Company

Aleman Brewing Company

3304 N. Knox Avenue
Chicago, Illinois 60639

alemanchicago.com

Established
2013

Leadership
Jim Moorehouse
Brad Zeller
Nate Albrecht
Josh Bearry

The Lawnmower Man

This cocktail was created specifically for a Beefsteak Banquet thrown at Aleman Brewing Company. It is the perfect refresher for a hedonistic feast.

Submitted by: Eric Rosentreter at Redemption Whiskey

Serve in a pint glass

Ingredients:

- 1 ½ ounce Redemption Rye
- ½ ounce elderflower liqueur
- ¾ ounce pineapple syrup
- ½ ounce lemon juice
- One dash Angostura Bitters
- Aleman's "LadiesMan" Wheat Ale

Preparation:

1. Build cocktail in pint glass over ice.
2. Add all ingredients other than wheat ale into glass.
3. Top off glass with wheat ale.
4. Stir and serve.

The Lawnmower Man
by Aleman Brewing Company

Aloha Beer Company (The HI Brau Room)

700 Queen Street
Honolulu, Hawaii 96813
(808) 544-1605

alohabeer.com

Established
2017

Leadership
Steve Sombrero - Owner
Dave Campbell - Brewmaster/Director of Operations

Barley Squared

Aloha Beer's HI Brau Room offers the eight core beers of the Aloha line up, with a cocktail program that is well-suited to the retro motif and sophisticated feel of the room.

Submitted by: Brad Miller, Beverage Director for Aloha Beer Company

Serve in an 11 ounce tumbler with a jigger for the spirit

Ingredients:
- IPA ice cube or globe*
- 2 ounces Suntory Toki
- Expressed orange swath

Preparation:
1. Place IPA Ice Cube and garnish with expressed orange swath.
2. Serve with 2 ounces Suntory Toki.
3. Spirit is poured over globe. As the cube/globe melts it slowly becomes the perfect "modified old fashioned."

*IPA Ice Cube or Globe – Aloha Beer uses its wort from its Hop Lei IPA. It is strained into preformed large cubes or globe trays. This wort makes for the perfect modified Old Fashioned as it contains malt sugars (sweet), hops (bitter) and water.

Alulu Brew Pub

2011 South Laflin Street
Chicago, Illinois 60608
(312) 600-9865

alulubrew.com
info@alulubrew.com

Established
2017

Leadership
Logan Helton, Brew Master
Nathan Bell, Beverage Director

Epishelf Marquee

This recipe emerged from the neighborhood from where the brew pub is based, Pilsen. The neighborhood has deep roots with its primarily Latin American population. The Epishelf Marquee is our answer to make a stronger smokier riff on a Michelada, a popular spicy Mexican beer and lime cocktail in the neighborhood.

Submitted by: Nathan Bell

Serve in an 8 ounce tulip glass

Ingredients:
- ¾ ounce mezcal
- ¼ ounce agave
- ¼ ounce vinegar based hot sauce (like Tabasco™)
- Squeeze of 2 lime wedges
- Epishelf Bridge Blonde Ale
- Lime wedge (for garnish)

Preparation:
1. Combine all ingredients other than beer and lime wedge for garnish in a pint glass.
2. Add ice, shake and strain into an 8 ounce tulip.
3. Top with Epishelf Bridge (blonde and golden ales work best).
4. Garnish with a lime wedge.

Anderson Valley Brewing Company

17700 Highway 253
Boonville, California 95415
(707) 895-2337

avbc.com

Established
1987

Leadership
Trey White

Holy Mule

Inspired by the Harry Nilsson song "Coconut," Steve Miller sought out to create a lime/coconut beer cocktail and decided to start by making a beer mule using our Holy Gose recipe and fresh ginger shrub he had in the refrigerator. Steve notes that this recipe also tastes great with unflavored vodka as well.

Submitted by: Steve Miller (aka Steinber Kimmie)

Serve in a rocks glass

Ingredients:

- 1 ½ ounces Skyy Vodka Coconut
- ½ ounce simple syrup
- ½ ounce fresh lime juice
- Ginger shrub
- 5 ounces The Kimmie, The Yink and The Holy Gose (Gose-style beer)

Preparation:

1. Combine all ingredients other than beer in a mixing glass filled with ice cubes.
2. Shake well and strain into a rocks glass.
3. Top with The Kimmie, The Yink and The Holy Gose.

Holy Mule
by Anderson Valley Brewing Company

Argyle Brewing Company

1 Main Street
Greenwich, New York 12834
Second tasting/taproom: 6 Broad Street
Cambridge, New York 12816
(518) 338-7405

argylebrewing.com
info@argylebrewing.com

Established
2013

Leadership
Christopher Castrio
Richard Thomas
Matthew Stewart

The Candy Corn

If you want to make this one really nice, you can rim the glass with a sugar/cinnamon or caramel sauce before you pour.

Submitted by: The Argyle Brewing Company

Serve in a pint glass

Ingredients:

- Pumpkin ale
- Oatmeal stout
- Cider (local/craft is best)

Preparation:

1. Just like candy corn, this is a triple-layered drink.
2. Start with the bottom layer by filling the glass ⅓ full with pumpkin ale.
3. Fill the middle ⅓ with oatmeal stout.
4. Top off the final layer with the cider.

The Candy Corn
by Argyle Brewing Company

Bear Bones Beer

43 Lisbon Street
Lewiston, Maine 04240
Second Location: 2 Cottage Street
Bridgton, Maine 04009
(207) 200-1324

bearbonesbeer.com
info@bearbonesbeer.com

Established
2013

Leadership
Adam Tuuri
Eben Dingman

Coffee & C.R.E.A.M.

The beer is a bourbon mash, aged with freshly toasted oak. A light gravity gives it a refreshing drinkablity. The flavor starts sweet with the bourbon mash and rounds out with the oak tannins on the finish. The suggested coffee is locally roasted organic Sumatran French roast cold brewed onsite and nitrogenated.

Submitted by: Bear Bones Beer

Serve in a pint glass

Ingredients:
- 8 ounces nitro cold brew coffee
- 8 ounces Double C.R.E.A.M. Beer (a bourbon mash beer)

Preparation:
1. The Double C.R.E.A.M. is poured first.
2. The coffee is carefully floated on top of it.

Coffee & C.R.E.A.M.
by Bear Bones Beer

Belching Beaver Tavern & Grill

302 East Broadway
Vista, California 92084
(760) 295-8599

belchingbeaver.com
info@belchingbeaver.com

Established
2016

Leadership
Tom Vogel, CEO
Dave Mobley, COO
Troy Smith, Brewmaster
Ralph Lizarraga, General Manager

The Bitter Truth

This beer cocktail is a take on a refreshing Mai Tai. As you enjoy this cocktail you'll be transported to your favorite beach. It's boozy, but very drinkable.

Submitted by: Byron Girdack – Creator

Serve in a pilsner glass

Ingredients:
- 1 ½ ounces gin
- ¾ ounces Aperol
- ¾ ounces Hop Liquor
- ¾ ounces St. Elder
- Belching Beaver Here Comes Mango IPA
- Fresh basil sprig

Preparation:
1. In a shaker with ice, add all ingredients other than beer and basil.
2. Shake and strain over fresh ice.
3. Top with Belching Beaver Here Comes Mango IPA, garnish with basil sprig and serve.

The Bitter Truth
by Belching Beaver Brewery Tavern & Grill

Cape Cod Beer

1336 Phinney's Lane
Hyannis, Massachusetts 02601
(508) 790-4200

capecodbeer.com
info@capecodbeer.com

Established
2004

Leadership
Beth & Todd Marcus

Cape & Islands Punch

This refreshing and light punch features Cape Cod Beer Beach Blonde Ale & Nantucket's 888 Cranberry Vodka.

Submitted by: Cape Cod Beer

Serve in a punch glass

Ingredients:
- 1 growler of Cape Cod Beer Beach Blonde Ale
- 1 bottle of 888 Cranberry Vodka
- 1 can of frozen pink lemonade
- Water
- Ice
- Cranberries and thinly sliced lemons, limes or oranges for garnish

Preparation:
1. You will use the lemonade can for measuring your ingredients into a large punch bowl.
2. Add one can of frozen pink lemonade.
3. Add Cape Cod Beer Beach Blonde Ale (fill the lemonade can three times).
4. Add cranberry vodka (fill the lemonade can once).
5. Add cold water (fill the lemonade can once).
6. Mix and add ice as desired.
7. Garnish with cranberries and thinly sliced lemons, limes or oranges.
8. A double batch is exactly 2 cans of frozen lemonade, 1 bottle of 888 cranberry vodka, one whole growler of beach blonde ale, and 2 cans of water.

Cape & Islands Punch
by Cape Cod Beer

Cinder Block Brewery

110 East 18th Avenue
North Kansas City, Missouri 64116

cinderblockbrewery.com

Established
2013

Leadership
Bryce Schaffter

Cherry Pit

Submitted by: Cinder Block Brewery

Serve in a highball glass

Ingredients:
- 1 ounce Reyka Vodka
- 1 ounce Velvet Falernum
- A few dashes of orange bitters
- Cherry cider
- Orange peel for garnish (optional)

Preparation:
1. Fill highball glass with ice.
2. Add vodka, Velvet Falernum and bitters to glass.
3. Stir with cocktail spoon and top with cherry cider.
4. Garnish with orange peel

Combustion Brewery & Taproom

80 W Church Street Suite 101
Pickerington, Ohio 43147
(614) 834-9595

combustionbrewing.com
info@combustionbrewing.com

Established
2017

Leadership
Keith and Sarah Jackson

Beer Mimosa Flight

Four beer-based mimosa cocktails to make a fun flight.

Submitted by: Combustion Brewery & Taproom

Serve in four half-pint glass

Devil in the Details Ingredients:
- 3 ounces Minutiae (Belgian Pale Ale)
- 2 ounces high quality freshly squeezed orange juice

Cranberry Lust Ingredients:
- 3 ounces Wanderlust (Blonde Ale)
- 2 ounces cranberry juice
- Splash of craft ginger beer

Malibu Barbie Ingredients:
- 3 ounces El Heffe (Traditional German Hefeweizen)
- 2 ounces high quality freshly squeezed orange juice

Grapefruit Moon Ingredients:
- 4 ½ ounces Ever The Other (Session IPA)
- ½ ounce high quality freshly squeezed grapefruit juice

Preparation:
1. Mix ingredients in glass for each cocktail.

Beer Mimosa Flight
by Combustion Brewery & Taproom

Crane Brewing Company

6515 Railroad Street
Raytown, Missouri 64133
(816) 743-4132

cranebrewing.com
chris@cranebrewing.com

Established
2015

Leadership
Chris Meyers
Michael Crane
Aaron Bryant
Randy Strange
Jason Louk

Orchards of Plenty

By stirring this drink, you can control dilution easier and avoid masking some of the nuances. It also keeps the mixture smooth and avoids creating little shards of ice that create nucleation points that cause the beer to lose carbonation too quickly.

Submitted by: Justin Jones

Serve in a 10 ounce Collins glass

Ingredients:
- 1 ½ ounces vanilla bean-infused Cardinal Calvados*
- ½ ounce Acidulated Donlin Blanc Vermouth**
- ¾ ounce Demerara Honey Syrup***
- 3 ounces Crane Brewing Orange Gose

Preparation:
1. In a mixing glass, combine vanilla infused Calvados, acidulated blanc vermouth, and demerara honey syrup.
2. Add ice, stir, strain into an ice-filled Collins glass.
3. Top with Crane Brewing Orange Gose

*Vanilla Bean-Infused Cardinal Calvados - Add one split Madagascar vanilla bean to one bottle 750ml bottle of Calvados and strain after 5-7 days.

**Acidulated Vermouth - Add five grams of powdered citric acid to ninety-five grams of Dolin Blanc and shake vigorously until citric powder mixes thoroughly into the solution.

***Demerara Honey Syrup - Mix 100 grams of Demerara Sugar with ten grams of honey and one-hundred grams of warm water. Shake mixture until honey and sugar mixes into solution.

Demented Brewing Company

600 Lincoln Boulevard
Middlesex, New Jersey 08846

dementedbrewing.com

Established
2015

Leadership
Tom Zuber, Owner

Orcus Old Fashioned

Liz Carrasquillo came up with this concept during one of the company's staff meetings. They usually infuse one of their beers weekly to have guests come in and try something different. Coming from a bartender background, she knew this cocktail would be a hit after tasting the beer fresh from the barrel. They went through 5 gallons in about two hours the first time it was served.

Submitted by: Liz Carrasquillo, Tasting Room Manager

Serve in a 13 ounce Belgian glass (like a snifter)

Ingredients*:
- Orcus (Scotch Ale aged for a year in Scotch Barrels)
- 1 ½ ounces of your preferred Scotch
- Angostura bitters
- 1 sugar cube
- Sliced orange (for garnish)
- Cocktail cherries (for garnish)

Preparation:
1. Place sugar cube in Belgian style beer glass and saturate with bitters.
2. Add Scotch and muddle until dissolved.
3. Fill glass with Orcus.
4. Garnish with orange slice and a cocktail cherry.

Per New Jersey law Demented Brewing notes they do not use any outside alcoholic beverages in the version of this served at the brewery. This was modified for the book.

Orcus Old Fashioned
by Demented Brewing Company

Deschutes Brewery

901 SW Simpson Avenue
Bend, Oregon 97702
(541) 385-8606

deschutesbrewery.com

Established
1988

Leadership
Gary Fish, Founder and Chairman
Deschutes Brewery is family and employee owned

Black Butte Bloody Mary

Submitted by: Deschutes Brewery

Serve in a pint glass

Ingredients:
- 5 ounces Black Butte Porter
- Old Bay Spice
- 4 ounces organic tomato juice
- 1 ounce J. Wilbur Bloody Mary Mix
- 1 ounce Blanco Tequila
- A beef stick, pickled green bean and pickled carrot (for garnish)

Preparation:
1. Wet rim of a 16 ounce pint glass with lemon.
2. Rim evenly with Old Bay Spice.
3. Combine tomato juice, Bloody Mary mix and tequila.
4. Add Black Butte Porter and garish with a beef stick, pickled green bean and pickled carrot.
5. Serve with a straw.

Black Butte Bloody Mary
by Deschutes Brewery

Dry Dock Brewing Company

15120 E. Hampden Avenue
Aurora, Colorado 80014
(303) 400-5606

drydockbrewing.com
info@drydockbrewing.com

Established
2005

Leadership
Michelle Reding
Kevin DeLange

Apricolada

Submitted by: Dry Dock Brewing Company

Serve in a tulip glass

Ingredients:
- 2 ounces white rum
- 1 ounce pineapple juice
- 1 ounce coconut cream
- 6 ounces Dry Dock Brewing Company's Apricot Blonde
- Pineapple wedge for garnish (optional)

Preparation:
1. Mix rum, pineapple juice, coconut cream, and ice in a cocktail shaker.
2. Strain into a tulip glass and top with 6 ounces of Dry Dock Brewing Company's Apricot Blonde.
3. Garnish with a pineapple wedge.

Apricolada

by Dry Dock Brewing Company

Empirical Brew Pub

1330 W Morse Avenue
Chicago, Illinois 60626
(773) 654-1561

empiricalbrewery.com
info@empiricalbrewery.com

Established
2017

Leadership
Bill Hurley
Steve Milford
Nikki Tyner

Gamma Mule

A straight forward riff on the Moscow Mule. Empirical uses their ginger wheat ale with fresh lime and the black/pink peppercorns replace the ginger beer perfectly. The whole package is uniquely its own. Try with bourbon, or rum, for a different feel.

Submitted by: Ryan Schofstal

Serve in a beer tulip/goblet

Ingredients:
- 1 ounce vodka
- 1 ounce lime juice
- 1 ounce simple syrup (equal parts sugar and water)
- 3 ounces Empirical Gamma Ray Ginger Wheat
- 1 lime wedge for garnish

Preparation:
1. Fill glass with ice.
2. Add vodka, lime and simple syrup.
3. Top off with ice (if needed) and top with beer.
4. Garnish with lime wedge and a straw.

Gamma Mule
by Empirical Brew Pub

Firetrucker Brewery

716 SW 3rd St
Ankeny, Iowa 50023
(515) 249-1069

firetrucker.com
info@firetrucker.com

Established
2014

Leadership
Dan Heiderscheit
Scott Kaven
Neil Zaugg
Liz Long, General Manager

German Chocolate Cake Porter

The German Chocolate Cake Porter was inspired by a favorite dessert of Firetrucker's bar manager. The caramel and nuts play well with the "roastiness" of the porter while the chocolate and coconut smooth it out. It's a dessert in (and on) a glass!

Submitted by: Liz Long

Serve in a beer tulip/goblet

Ingredients:
- Caramel sauce
- Ground pecans
- Shredded coconut
- ½ teaspoon of cocoa powder
- Pumper Truck Porter

Preparation:
1. Swirl caramel sauce in a beer tulip glass.
2. Dip rim in caramel sauce.
3. Dip rim in mixture of half ground pecans and half coconut shreds.
4. Add cocoa powder to glass.
5. Top with Pumper Truck Porter.

German Chocolate Cake Porter
by Firetrucker Brewery

Foothills Brewing

638 W. 4th Street
Winston-Salem, North Carolina 27101
(336) 777-3348

foothillsbrewing.com
hello@foothillsbrewing.com

Established
2005

Leadership
Jamie and Sarah Bartholomaus
Matt and Meredith Masten

The Pacific Jade

The name of the cocktail comes from the dominant hop in Foothills Brewing's Jade IPA. Pacific Jade hops are grown exclusively in New Zealand, and are known for their pepper and citrus notes. Those flavors work well with the lavender and coriander in Sutler's Gin, from a local distillery here in Winston-Salem.

Submitted by: Nicole LaCarrubba - Bar Manager

Serve in a 12 ounce pilsner glass

Ingredients:
- 1 ½ ounces Sutler's Gin
- 1 ½ ounces Foothills Jade IPA
- ¼ ounce fresh lime juice
- ¼ ounce housemade rosemary simple syrup*
- ¾ ounce grapefruit juice

Preparation:
1. In a shaker combine gin, lime juice, simple syrup, and grapefruit juice over ice.
2. Shake well, strain into pilsner glass filled with ice.
3. Stir in Jade IPA and garnish with lime wedge and rosemary sprig.

*Housemade Rosemary Simple Syrup:
Simply combine one cup water, one cup sugar, and four large rosemary sprigs in a saucepan and bring to a boil for one minute. Turn off heat and let steep for 45 minutes. Strain the cooled syrup into a sterilized, airtight glass jar. Can be kept in refrigerator for up to 2 weeks.

The Pacific Jade
by Foothills Brewing

Forbidden Root Restaurant and Brewery

1746 West Chicago Avenue
Chicago, Illinois 60622
(312) 929-2202

forbiddenroot.com

Established
2015

Leadership
Robert Finkel, Owner

The Rake

Submitted by: Forbidden Root

Serve in a rocks glass

Ingredients:
- 1 ounce Old Forester Signature Bourbon
- 1 ounce Génépy Des Alpes
- ½ ounce fresh lemon juice
- ½ ounce pink peppercorn syrup*
- 1 dash Boker's Bitters
- 1 dash Hopped Grapefruit Bitters
- 2 ounces Forbidden Root "WPA"
- Lemon swath for garnish
- Ground pink peppercorn for garnish

Preparation:
1. Take all ingredients other than beer and lemon swath and put into a cocktail shaker with ice.
2. Give it a quick shake.
3. Strain into a rocks glass with ice. Pour beer into glass. Garnish with a swath of lemon and ground pink peppercorn on top.

*Pink Peppercon Syrup:
Combine 4 ounces boiling water with 4 ounces sugar and 1 ½ ounces ground pink peppercorn (by volume). Stir together and let sit until cooled. Strain and store in the refrigerator.

Friendship Brewing Company

100 Pitman Avenue
Wentzville, Missouri 63385
(636) 856-9300

friendshipbrewingcompany.com
friendshipbrewingcompany@yahoo.com

Established
2015

Leadership
Brian Nolan
Mike Wood

Friendship Recovery

Friendship Brewing has a build-your-own bloody Mary bar on Sundays. They note their brewing staff has been making beer together for years and enjoy "research and development" with their craft beer products, so they've needed a little spicy recovery on more than a few Sundays. Offering a bloody Mary spicy beer has proven to be a fun reward for themselves and their beloved patrons.

Submitted by: Friendship Brewing Company

Serve in a pint glass

Ingredients (makes 2 ½ gallons):
- Rasmanian Devil Beer (raspberry/jalapeno) or Wasabwitu Beer (wasabi/wheat)
- V8 Bloody Mary Mix or Zing Zang Bloody Mary Mix
- 2 heaping tablespoons of freshly grated horseradish
- ½ cup pickle juice (Tabasco™ pickles suggested)
- Fresh ground pink peppercorn (to taste)
- Dash of celery salt
- Cajun spice (optional for glass rimming)
- Premium vodka, single or double shot

Preparation:
1. In a 2 ½ gallon container, mix ⅓ beer and ⅔ bloody Mary mix.
2. Add horseradish, pickle juice, peppercorns, celery salt and stir.
3. Serve in a Cajun spice rimmed pint glass (with vodka).

Half Day Brewing Co.

200 Village Green
Lincolnshire, Illinois 60069
(847) 821-6933

halfdaybrewing.com

Established
2016

Leadership
Mark Zych
Scott Ward

Iron Horse Coffee Porter Café

Submitted by: Half Day Brewing Co.

Serve in a 12 ounce cocktail glass

Ingredients:
- 1 ounce Patrón XO Café
- 1 ounce Frangelico
- Half Day Brewing Iron Horse Porter
- Splash of cream
- Chocolate covered coffee beans (for garnish)

Preparation:
1. Add ice to a 12 ounce cocktail glass and build drink in glass.
2. Pour Patrón and Frangelico in glass.
3. Top glass with porter beer (leaving room for cream).
4. Float cream on top.
5. Garnish with chocolate covered coffee beans.

Iron Horse Coffee Porter Café
by Half Day Brewing Co.

Heavy Seas Alehouse Baltimore

1300 Bank Street, Suite 201
Baltimore, Maryland 21231
(410) 522-0850

heavyseasalehouse.com/Baltimore.html
arnold@heavyseasalehouse.com

Established
2011

Leadership
Arnold Dion, General Manager

Southern Cross

Arnold Dion notes, "Because the drink contains Crossbones and tequila, the name, Southern Cross was a no brainer."

Submitted by: Arnold Dion, General Manager

Serve in a pilsner glass

Ingredients:

- 2 ounces Heavy Seas Crossbones
- 1 ounce Dulce Vida grapefruit tequila
- ½ ounce Effen Vodka
- Sanpellegrino Pompelo (about 3 ounces)
- Lime wedge (for garnish)

Preparation:

1. Top off 10 ounce pilsner glass with ice.
2. Add Dulce Vida and Effen, then Crossbones.
3. Pour into shaker and blend.
4. Pour drink back into glass.
5. Top with Pompelo.
6. Garnish with lime wedge and serve with tall, black straw.

Southern Cross
by Heavy Seas Alehouse Baltimore

Jolly Pumpkin Artisan Ales

2319 Bishop Circle East
Dexter, Michigan 48130
(734) 792-9124

jollypumpkin.com

Established
2004

Leadership
Ron Jeffries, Founder and Chief Squeegee Operator

Bam Shandy

This drink was inspired by summer days on the lake in Michigan. It uses Jolly Pumpkin's Farmhouse Ale as a base and adds some seasonal tropical and citrus flavors to create a refreshing cocktail for day or night.

Submitted by: Keith Martin, Taphouse Manager

Serve in a beer tulip/goblet

Ingredients:

- 8 ounces Bam Biere Farmhouse Ale
- 2 ounces pineapple juice
- 1 ounce simple syrup
- ½ ounce lemon juice
- Splash of lemon-lime soda
- Lemon wheel for garnish

Preparation:

1. Combine juices, and simple syrup into a large goblet.
2. Scoop ice about one-third full into glass.
3. Top with Bam Biere.
4. Add a splash of lemon-lime soda and garnish with a lemon wheel.

Bam Shandy
by Jolly Pumpkin Artisan Ales

Left Hand Brewing Company

1265 Boston Avenue
Longmont, Colorado 80501
(303) 772-0258

lefthandbrewing.com

Established
1993

Leadership
Eric Wallace
Dick Doore

Good Juju Moscow Mule

Submitted by: Left Hand Brewing Company

Serve in a copper mug

Ingredients:
- 2 ounces of quality vodka
- 3 ounces of Good Juju ginger pale ale beer
- Juice of half a lime
- Lime wheel (for garnish)

Preparation:
1. Squeeze half a fresh lime into the mug.
2. Add vodka.
3. Fill the mug with crushed ice or small cubes so it mounds on top.
4. Pour Left Hand Good Juju ginger pale ale over ice.
5. Garnish with a lime wheel and enjoy!

Good Juju Moscow Mule
by Left Hand Brewing Company

Logboat Brewing Co.

504 Fay Street
Columbia, Missouri 65201
(573) 397-6786

logboatbrewing.com

Established
2104

Leadership
Tyson Hunt
Judson Ball
Andrew Sharp

Turtle Power!

Knowing not everyone is a big beer fan, Nick wanted to have fun, creative drinks that incorporated their beers... and Ninja Turtles rule (of course).

Submitted by: Nick Hardy/Logboat Brewing Co. - Creator of Turtle Power!

Serve in a Collins glass

Ingredients:
- 1 ounce Pickney Bend Vodka
- ½ ounce fresh-squeezed organic lemon juice
- ½ ounce St. Germain Elderflower Liqueur
- 2 ounces citrusy India Pale Ale beer (Suggested: Logboat Brewing's Snapper IPA)
- 2 ounces semisweet ruby red grapefruit juice
- 3 to 4 drops grapefruit bitters

Preparation:
1. In a shaker pint, add lemon juice, grapefruit juice, grapefruit bitters, St. Germain Elderflower liqueur and vodka to the shaker.
2. Shake and strain over ice in a Collins glass (tall, skinny glass tumbler).
3. Top with IPA.
4. Garnish with a slice of fresh grapefruit.

Turtle Power!
by Logboat Brewing Co.

Maui Brewing Co. / Waikiki Pub

2300 Kalakaua Avenue
Honolulu, Hawaii 96815
(808) 843-BREW (2739)

mauibrewingco.com
pr@mauibrewingco.com

Established
2005

Leadership
Garrett Marrero, Founder/CEO
Melanie Oxley, Founder/COO

Bahama Mana

A take on a tiki classic.

Submitted by: Damon Baker, Lead Bartender

Serve in a Hefeweizen glass

Ingredients:
- 1 ounce Koloa Coconut Rum
- 1 ounce Old Lahaina Silver Rum
- ¾ ounce freshly squeezed orange juice
- 2 ounces Maui Brewing Co. Pineapple Mana Wheat
- ¾ ounce BG Reynolds Grenadine with Hibiscus
- 4 pineapple leaves
- 1 Luxardo maraschino cherry
- 1 bamboo knotted pick

Preparation:
1. In a Hefeweizen glass, add BG Reynolds Grenadine and then add ice.
2. Once ice is added, layer Koloa Coconut Rum and Old Lahaina Silver Rums.
3. Add fresh orange juice and top with 2 oz. of Maui Brewing Co Pineapple Mana Wheat.
4. Garnish: Flare out 4 ripe pineapple leaves, run the bamboo pick through the cherry then the leaves, set garnish in the cocktail with the base of the leaves entering the beverage.

Bahama Mana
by Maui Brewing Co. / Waikiki Pub

Midnight Sun Brewing Company

8111 Dimond Hook Drive
Anchorage, Alaska 99507

midnightsunbrewing.com
info@midnightsunbrewing.com

Established
1995

Leadership
Mark Staples
Barb Miller
Gary Busse

Trick'd Out Old Fashioned

You can use whatever bourbon you like for this one, but the team at Midnight Sun prefers something with a kick, like Booker's.

Submitted by: Darcy Kniefel

Serve in a bucket

Ingredients:

- 1 ½ ounces bourbon
- 3 ounces Trickster Belgian Ale with Pumpkin and Spices
- 2 dashes bitters
- 1 orange wedge
- 1 Luxardo maraschino cherry

Preparation:

1. Muddle bitters, orange and cherry.
2. Top with ice and bourbon.
3. Shake lightly to combine and top with Trickster.

Outlaw Brewing Company

215 Scotland Road
Winchester, New Hampshire 03470

theoutlawbrewingcompany.com
info@theoutlawbrewingcompany.com

Established
2017

Leadership
Rick and Sarah Horton

The Ultimate Enticement

This recipe is all about the local flavors from Winchester, New Hampshire. It's a pairing of the local beer and gin. Robert (the owner of New England Sweetwater Distillery) and Rick (the owner of The Outlaw Brewing Company) consider themselves "brothers in alcohol."

Submitted by: Rick Horton

Serve in a martini glass

Ingredients:
- 3 ounces Outlaw Brewing Company American Blonde Ale
- 3 ounces New England Sweetwater Distillery Gin
- 3 olives stuffed with jalapenos
- 1 teaspoon jalapeno juice
- Ice cubs

Preparation:
1. Add all ingredients in glass and top with ice.
2. Stir gently and serve.

Red Clay Brewing Company

704 N. Railroad Avenue
Opelika, Alabama 36801
(334) 737-5409

redclaybrewingcompany.com
info@redclaybrewingcompany.com

Established
2014

Leadership
John Corbin
Kerry McGinnis
Stephen Harle

Red Clay Peach Sour

This beer drink is even enjoyed by the non-beer drinkers that come into the brewery taproom.

Submitted by: John Corbin

Serve in a 16 ounce Belgian teardrop glass

Ingredients:
- 1 ½ ounces peach nectar
- 1 ounce agave nectar
- 2 dashes of Angostura Bitters
- Drymarchon Sour (Berliner Weisse beer)
- 1 peach sliver (for garnish)

Preparation:
1. Pour the peach and agave nectars along with the Angostura bitters in the bottom of the glass.
2. Add a small amount of the Drymarchon Sour and stir.
3. Fill Glass to the top it off with Drymarchon Sour.
4. Float a sliver of peach on top.

Revolution Brewing

3340 N. Kedzie Avenue
Chicago, Illinois 60618
(773) 588-2267

revbrew.com
info@revbrew.com

Established
2010

Leadership
Josh Deth

Kentucky Rosa

Rosa is Revolution's summer seasonal offering, brewed with real dried hibiscus flowers. It's developed quite a following in Chicago centered around the cocktails made with it. It's a great beer for the summer, but its versatility in cocktails has opened a lot of doors to retail accounts that might otherwise turn their nose up at beer.

Submitted by: Revolution Brewing

Serve in a rocks glass

Ingredients:
- Revolution Rosa Hibiscus Ale
- 1 ½ ounces bourbon or rye
- ½ ounce simple syrup
- ¾ ounce lemon juice
- Lemon twist

Preparation:
1. Combine whiskey, lemon juice and simple syrup in glass.
2. Add ice and stir.
3. Fill with ice and top with Revolution Rosa Hibiscus Ale.
4. Express lemon twist and garnish with lemon twist.

Kentucky Rosa
by Revolution Brewing

SanTan Brewing Company

8 S. San Marcos Place
Chandler, Arizona 85225
(480) 917-8700

santanbrewing.com
info@santanbrewing.com

Established
2007

Leadership
Anthony Canecchia, Founder & Brewmaster
Jamie Hoffman, Managing Partner

SanTan Arizona Mule

A "SanTan Brewing Company" twist on the popular Moscow Mule.

Submitted by: SanTan Brewing Company

Serve in a 16 ounce goblet

Ingredients:

- 1 ½ ounces SanTan Sacred Stave Kaffir Lime Vodka
- 1 teaspoon freshly squeezed lime juice
- 1 ½ ounces house made ginger lime syrup
- Club soda
- Splash of SunSpot Gold (golden ale)
- Lime wheel for garnish

Preparation:

1. Pour vodka, lime juice and ginger lime syrup in goblet filled with crushed ice.
2. Fill with club soda (leaving room for splash of golden ale)
3. Add splash of SunSpot Gold.
4. Add lime wheel for garnish.

Square One Brewery

1727 Park Avenue
St. Louis, Missouri 63104
(314) 231-2537

squareonebrewery.com / spiritsofstlouisdistillery.com
info@squareonebrewery.com

Established
2006 (Restaurant/Brewery)
2008 (Distillery)

Leadership
Steve Neukomm, Owner
John Witte, Director of Beverage Operations
Robert Aguilar, Head Mixologist
Dave Wohldmann, Head Brewer
Kenny Franklin, Head Distiller

Breakfast Beer

The perfect balance of sweetness and coffee flavors to complement Square One's traditional dry Irish Stout. The ideal beer cocktail to sip when sitting on Square One's (or yours) gorgeous patio enjoying Sunday Brunch!

Submitted by: Robert Aguilar

Serve in a half-pint (8 ounce) glass

Ingredients:

- ¾ ounce Vermont Night (whiskey base liqueur infused with winter spices, citrus zest, and maple syrup)
- ¾ ounce house-made chocolate liqueur
- ½ ounce cold-brew espresso
- Square One's Irish Stout
- Luxardo Maraschino Cherry (for garnish)

Preparation:

1. Shake the liqueurs and espresso without ice.
2. Pour the liqueurs into an 8 oz. glass and top with Square One's Irish Stout.
3. Garnish with the Luxardo Maraschino Cherry

Breakfast Beer
by Square One Brewery

Sun King Brewery

135 North College Avenue
Indianapolis, Indiana 46202
(317) 602-3702

sunkingbrewing.com
info@sunkingbrewing.com

Established
2009

Leadership
Clay Robinson, Co-Founder/Owner
Dave Colt, Co-Founder/Owner

Pachangarita

Submitted by: Steven Unrue, Sun King Culinary Director

Serve in a pint or margarita glass

Ingredients:
- 3 ounces silver tequila
- 1 ounce Cointreau
- 12 ounces Pachanga (Mexican-Style lager)
- ⅓ cup lime juice
- ⅓ cup simple syrup
- 2 slices jalapeño
- 1 lime round (for garnish)
- Salt (for rim)
- Ice

Preparation:
1. Salt the rim of the glass and set aside.
2. Lightly muddle one jalapeño slice in a shaker
3. Add ice and the rest of the ingredients other than the beer, second jalapeño slice and lime round into the shaker.
4. Shake vigorously and strain into glass with fresh ice.
5. Top with Mexican lager, garnish side of glass with jalapeño slice and lime round and serve.

Pachangarita
by Sun King Brewery

ThirstyBear Brewing Company

661 Howard Street
San Francisco, California 94105

thirstybear.com

Established
1996

Leadership
Ron Silberstein

Beer Cocktail #18

For this cocktail, the goal of Shina Kang was to keep the ingredients simple and really play up the main flavor components of their Tolstoy's Inkwell Russian Imperial Stout. She was looking for a base liquor that wasn't as high in alcohol because the Stout is a high alcohol beer. The Amaro Ciociaro is an earthy, herbal and bittersweet liqueur that along with the Xocolatl (chocolate) Mole bitters really highlight the robust, malty and bittersweet chocolate flavors of the Stout and the (cold) espresso is added to emphasize the roasted barley notes in the beer.

Submitted by: Shina Kang

Serve in a coupe glass

Ingredients:
- 2 ounces Tolstoy's Inkwell Russian Imperial Stout
- 1 ounce of Amaro Ciociaro
- 1 ounce of cold espresso
- Roughly 4 drops of Xocolatl Mole Bitters

Preparation:
1. In ice in a shaker, combine all ingredients and shake vigorously.
2. Strain into a coupe.
3. This cocktail should have a nice frothy head.

Beer Cocktail #18
by ThirstyBear Brewing Company

Twisted Spike Brewing Company

1 Northwest 10th Street
Oklahoma City, Oklahoma 73103
(405) 297-9961

twistedspike.com
bruce@twistedspike.com

Established
2016

Leadership
Bruce and Donna Sanchez

Beermosa

Submitted by: Twisted Spike Brewing Company

Serve in a Belgian teardrop glass

Ingredients:
- Twisted Spike Brewing Company Golden Spike Saison
- Orange juice

Preparation:
1. In the glass combine 75% beer and 25% orange juice.

Beermosa
by Twisted Spike Brewing Company

Voodoo Brewery

834 Bessemer Street, Meadville, Pennsylvania 16335
215 Arch Street, Meadville, Pennsylvania 16335
101 Boston Store Place, Erie Pennsylvania 16501
205 East 9th Avenue, Homestead, Pennsylvania 15120
(814) 337-3676

voodoobrewery.com
info@voodoobrewery.com

Established
2005

Leadership
Employee-owned

MAKERS OF ARTISAN BEERS
MEADVILLE | ERIE | HOMESTEAD

Met-Mosa

Submitted by: The employee owners of Voodoo Brewery

Serve in a tulip glass

Ingredients:
- Voodoo Brewery Gran Met Belgian Tripel
- Fresh Orange Juice (pineapple or mango juice may be substituted)

Preparation:
1. Fill glass halfway with beer.
2. Top off with juice.

Resources

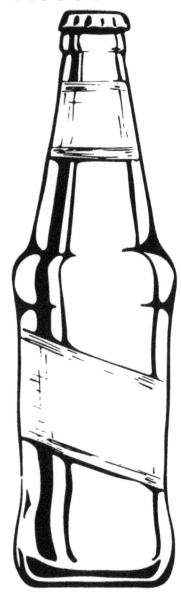

Websites of Featured Breweries

I encourage you to learn more about these businesses and what makes them so special. To make your job a little easier, here's a recap of the websites for each:

7 Mile Brewery – *7milebrew.com*

16 Mile Brewing Company – *16milebrewery.com*

32 North Brewing Company – *32northbrew.com*

Abbey of the Holy Goats Brewery – *abbeyoftheholygoats.com*

Absolution Brewing Company – *absolutionbrewingcompany.com*

Aleman Brewing Company – *alemanchicago.com*

Aloha Beer Company – *alohabeer.com*

Alulu Brew Pub – *alulubrew.com*

Anderson Valley Brewing Company – *avbc.com*

Argyle Brewing Company – *argylebrewing.com*

Bear Bones Beer – *bearbonesbeer.com*

Belching Beaver Brewery – *belchingbeaver.com*

Cape Cod Beer – *capecodbeer.com*

Cinder Block Brewery – *cinderblockbrewery.com*

Combustion Brewery & Taproom – *combustionbrewing.com*

Crane Brewing Company – *cranebrewing.com*

Demented Brewing Company – *dementedbrewing.com*

Deschutes Brewery – *deschutesbrewery.com*

Dry Dock Brewing Company – *drydockbrewing.com*

Empirical Brew Pub – *empiricalbrewery.com*

Firetrucker Brewery – *firetrucker.com*

Foothills Brewing – *foothillsbrewing.com*

Forbidden Root Restaurant and Brewery – *forbiddenroot.com*

Friendship Brewing Company – *friendshipbrewingcompany.com*

Half Day Brewing Co. – *halfdaybrewing.com*

Heavy Seas Alehouse Baltimore – *heavyseasalehouse.com/Baltimore.html*

Jolly Pumpkin Artisan Ales – *jollypumpkin.com*

Left Hand Brewing Company – *lefthandbrewing.com*

Logboat Brewing Co. – *logboatbrewing.com*

Maui Brewing Co. – *mauibrewingco.com*

Midnight Sun Brewing – *midnightbrewing.com*

The Outlaw Brewing Company – *theoutlawbrewingcompany.com*

Red Clay Brewing Company – *redclaybrewingcompany.com*

Revolution Brewing – *revbrew.com*

SanTan Brewing Company – *santanbrewing.com*

Square One Brewery – *squareonebrewery.com*

Sun King Brewery – *sunkingbrewing.com*

Twisted Spike Brewing Company – *twistedspike.com*

ThirstyBear Brewing Company – *thirstybear.com*

Voodoo Brewery – *voodoobrewery.com*

Photo Credits

All photographs in the sections of each business featured have been utilized with permission from the respective companies with the following exceptions:

Abbey of the Holy Goats Brewery
The Brewery – Keith Godfrey

Logboat Brewing Co.
Nick/Turtle Power Cocktail – Inside Columbia Magazine
Logboat Brewing Company Exterior – Judson Ball

Square One Brewery
Photo of Square One/St. Louis Skyline - @stl_from_above

About the Authors

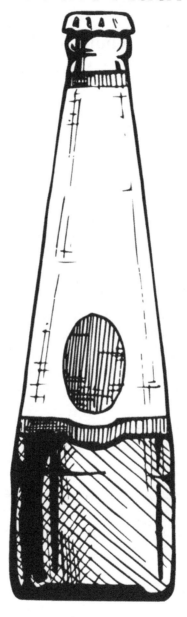

About the Authors
Steve Akley

Steve Akley is a lifelong St. Louis resident. His approach to writing is very simple. He knows his passion comes from topics he enjoys so he sticks to what he knows best. In addition to books, he also publishes a monthly email magazine called Bourbon Zeppelin and is a cohost of two popular bourbon-themed podcasts, The Bourbon Show, The Bourbon Daily and Bourbon History.

He maintains an author's page on Amazon.com. Just search his name on the site. He can be reached via email: info@steveakley.com.

Find Steve on Social Media

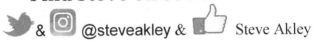 & @steveakley & Steve Akley

About the Authors (continued)

Lee Ann Sciuto

Lee Ann, aka Punky the Intern, has known Steve since she was 9 years old. Besides helping Steve with the Bourbon Zeppelin, or a new book, she keeps busy trying to keep up with her daughter. She currently lives in St. Louis with her husband, daughter, and dog.

Steve's Other Works

Bourbon Mixology Series

Be sure to check out all of the offerings in Steve's best-selling **Bourbon Mixology** series!

Podcasting

Steve serves as the lead writer, producer and co-host for two of the top ranked bourbon-themed podcasts: The Bourbon Show, The Bourbon Daily and Bourbon History. Check them out on iTunes, your favorite podcast provider or his podcast company's website: *abvnetwork.com*.

Special Thanks

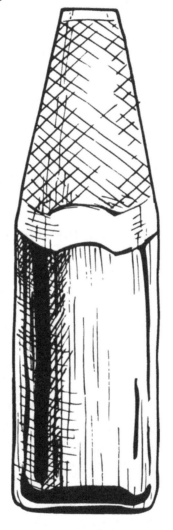

Much Appreciation for Those That Helped

To my wife Amy, and my sister-in-law Lee Ann Sciuto for their help in editing this book.

Thanks to our daughters Cat (Steve) and Tessa (Lee Ann) for just being themselves.

Hats off to Mark Hansen (*mappersmark@gmail.com*) for the great cover design. He's the greatest graphic artist you will ever find!

The following individuals from the featured companies not only couldn't have been nicer, without their help this book would not have been possible:

Meg Herbert/SanTan Brewing Company, Ashley Vander Meeden/Left Hand Brewing Company, Jordan Miller/Deschutes Brewery, Steve Miller/Anderson Valley Brewing Company, Arnold Dion/Heavy Seas Alehouse Baltimore, Judson Bell/Logboat Brewing Co., Voodoo Brewery, Erin Hamrick/Dry Dock Brewing Company, Anna Oliver/Revolution Brewing, Ray Goodrich/Foothills Brewing, Bear Bones Beer, Marsha Hansen/Maui Brewing Co., Steve Peterson/32 North Brewing Company, Chris Meyers/Crane Brewing Company, Ben Smego/Tap House Management Group, Brad Zeller/Aleman Brewing Company, Brad Miller/Aloha Beer Company, Amanda Kaiser/Cape Cod Beer, Haley McHenry/Belching Beaver Brewery, Mark Demberger/7 Mile Brewery, Shina Kang/ThirstyBear Brewing Company, Katharine Uhrich/Forbidden Root Restaurant and

Brewery, Robert Aguilar/Square One Brewery, Asia Coleman/Abbey of the Holy Goats Brewery, Liz Long/Firetrucker Brewery, Nigel Heath/Absolution Brewing Company, Ryan Schofstal/Empirical Brew Pub, Sarah Hearn/Cinder Block Brewery, Keith Martin/Jolly Pumpkin Artisan Ales, Sarah Jackson/Combustion Brewery & Taproom, Rick & Sarah Horton/The Outlaw Brewing Company, Bruce Sanchez/Twisted Spike Brewing Company, Brian Nolan/Friendship Brewing Company, John Corbin/Red Clay Brewing Company, the team at Midnight Sun Brewing, Nathan Bell/Alulu Brew Pub, Elizabeth Belange/Sun King Brewery, Liz Carasquillo/Demented Brewing Company, Angelina Idler/16 Mile Brewing Company & Christophper Castro/Argyle Brewing Company.

Lastly, lots of love for my father, Larry Akley. He's always with us in spirit.

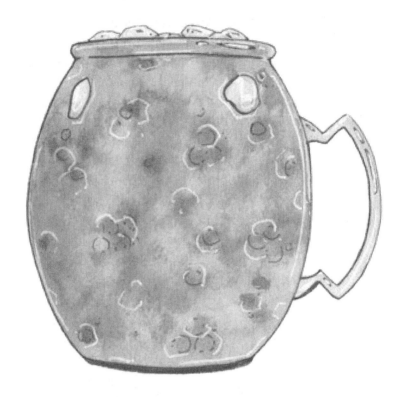

THE END

Made in the USA
Monee, IL
18 December 2019